SIMPLICITY
IN MIND

Published by Julia Trops ISBN 978-0-9813363-1-2

Designed and compiled by Julia Trops
Edited by Rebekah Wilkinson

Cover artwork by Sandra (Sam) Windsor "Sisters of the Sea"

Photo credit Julia Trops for artworks of Sam Windsor, Dianne Schnieders, Ralf Rohrlack, Rebekah Wilkinson

Font: title page: Herculanum
Paragraphs: Arial
Headings: Herculanum

"In art, the hand can never execute anything higher than the heart can inspire."

Ralph Waldo Emerson

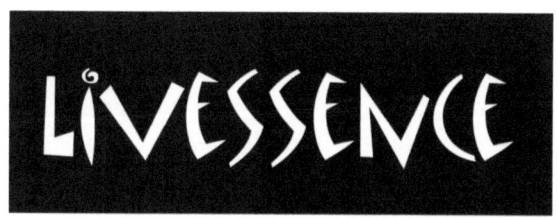

society for figurative artists and models

ABOUT LIVESSENCE

We are going in to our sixth year as a non profit organization, and the eighth year that drawing has been running at the Rotary Centre for the Arts. Little did I know when I started the drawing sessions in 2003 that we would progress so far!

It is to our artists that credit must go. Our artists are our volunteers, our visionaries, our advocates. Our artists may have meandering paths, their attendance weaving in and out, but one can never run away from drawing or our addiction and attachment to the human form. No matter how hard we try!

Thank you so much to our past and current board members, we would not be where we are without you! J.T.

2005
Norman Goddard
Isabelle Gambouras
Laura Widmer
Victor Marko
Julia Trops

2006
Norman Goddard
Isabelle Gambouras
Laura Widmer
Victor Marko
Julia Trops

2007
Isabelle Gambouras
Margaret Gleig
Ralf Rohrlack
Pat Higgins
Julia Trops

2008
Elizabeth Hodgkinson
Margaret Gleig
Hylton Harrington
Pat Higgins
Ralf Rohrlack
Julia Trops

2009
Tina Siddiqui
Elizabeth Hodgkinson
Christina Leinemann Knittel
Rebekah Wilkinson
Tina Schnellert
Hylton Harrington
Julia Trops

2010
Tina Siddiqui
Dianne Schnieders
Rebekah Wilkinson
Tina Schnellert
Sandra Bradshaw
Julia Trops

A WELCOME TO OUR EXHIBITION

It is instinctive for humans to draw figures going all the way back to cave art. Keeping that flame alive, with beauty in simplicity in mind, Livessence presents it's biggest endeavour, Stick Figures.

The rhythmic flow of the human body on the surfaces of the 30 paintings are as delightful as they diverse in styles and execution. It has been a challenge to draw/paint outside the comfort zone of our individual preferences, but the response has created a body of work that has allowed us to discover our own power. Minimalism is a monumental task, to strip the figures down to their fundamental features the results are evident in this collection. Our society hopes to reach out and engage the community as we have often heard remarks of the like ....."I can only draw stick figures".

Many thanks to our Exhibition Chair, Rebekah Wilkinson for her untiring efforts in putting this show together and to our founding member, Julia Trops for her support, presence and valuable input for the society.

Members and non members are thankful for the opportunity to be able to draw figures from life as we welcome artists of all levels to experience and enjoy this adventure. The Livessence Society for Figurative Artists and Models aims to promote camaraderie and fellowship as well as provide resources, learning and practice opportunities to artists and models interested in art based on the human figure. We are friendly folk with diverse backgrounds and varying levels of artistic experience and expertise working in a wide variety of media. Exciting workshops and numerous shows are some of the other things we do as a group.

Tina Siddiqui
President

FOREWORD

What is a stick figure really?

A circle for a head, a line for the body, an inverted "v" for the legs, and a couple of lines for arms make up the preconceived graphic image of a stick figure learned in childhood. But who defines what is a stick figure? Is it an already preconceived notion of a graphic image? Or, is it a figure drawn with simple lines? How far into detailing can you go before the image is no longer a stick figure? And, what about a stick figure as a metaphor, allegory or symbol?

All these questions came into play with the issuing of this challenge. It started out as a generic theme to get artists thinking and creating, but in the end, it turned into more of a challenge than what they had bargained for. In the end, some artists choose not to participate as they realized it was too far outside their creative comfort zone.

Simplifying isn't necessarily easier. If you remove the detail, the difficulty comes in conveying and capturing the intended message. If you remove the detail, where is the visual interest?

For all those people, envious of artists, who claim they can only "draw stick figures", maybe they are further along than they think.

Rebekah Wilkinson
Exhibitions Chairman

SIMPLICITY IN MIND

CALL TO ARTISTS

The exhibition proposal given to our Livessence members:

As figurative artists, we are often complimented on our ability to capture the human body within our pieces of art. Non-artists often comment that they can only draw stick men. But what they don't realize is that "only drawing stick men" can be a beginning point to further exploration and creativity within visual arts. With the show theme of "Stick Figures", we want to open this visual dialogue with the greater public to showcase what can be created from stick figures.

When you think of stick figures, cartoon characters automatically come to mind. But if this simple image is pushed with artistic flair and artistic textures or techniques, great pieces of art can be developed. Stick figures can show movement and emotions just by simple strokes. Stick figures can be used in graphic patterns of colours or pushed to abstraction. Stick figures can hide in nature or in the everyday and just need to be brought to the attention of the viewer in an unique, creative way. Stick figures can tell a story or be allegorical.

In addition to engaging the public, this show theme is intended to push the creativity of the Livessence membership to develop art beyond anatomy learned and discovered through weekly drawing sessions. What does the theme "stick figure" mean to you? How would you draw a "stick figure" in an unique and creative way?

Rebekah Wilkinson
Exhibitions Chairman

THE ARTISTS

SANDRA (SAM) WINDSOR

Cocktail Party
Ink & watercolour, 22x15

 At first the idea of stick figures was a challenge for me.........
since my style of drawing is more on the realistic side...............
I had to think back when I was a child on how I drew people and animals...........more on the animated side I would say.........................
the Cocktail Party idea came from back when my parents used to have twice yearly big parties.............
I remember them being fun and the people so colourful and some were real characters..........always an entertaining time for me.........
All the people in the cocktail party are family or friends including the German Shepherd dog. This drawing took me awhile to produce since I tried hard to keep lines straight with just enough detail ......
as well as the character of each person.

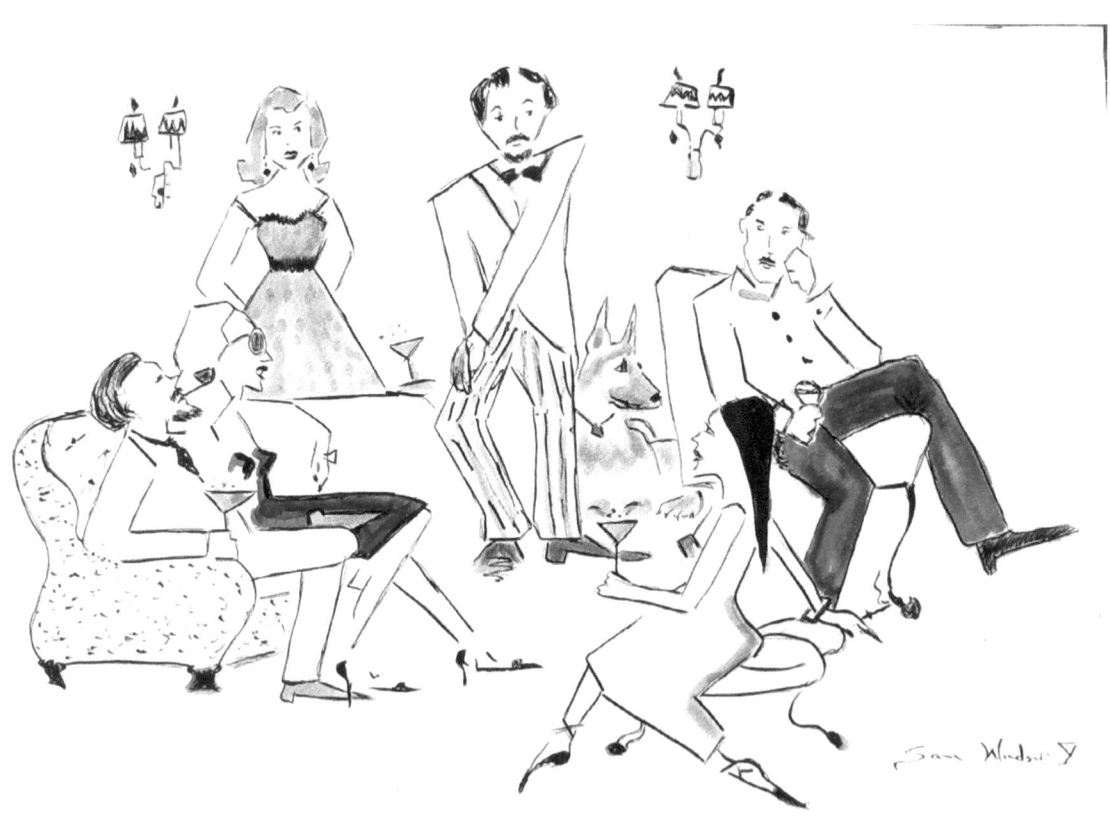

Sisters of the Sea
Ink & watercolour, 15x10

The Sisters Of The Sea drawing ....
came from memories of spending all our summers out on the family boat around the gulf islands........
as children my sisters and I ran about the islands beaches like a little gaggle of gypsies...........
playing and pretending the large kelp washed ashore on the rocks were stranded mermaids..........
we would drag them back into the water to set them free.

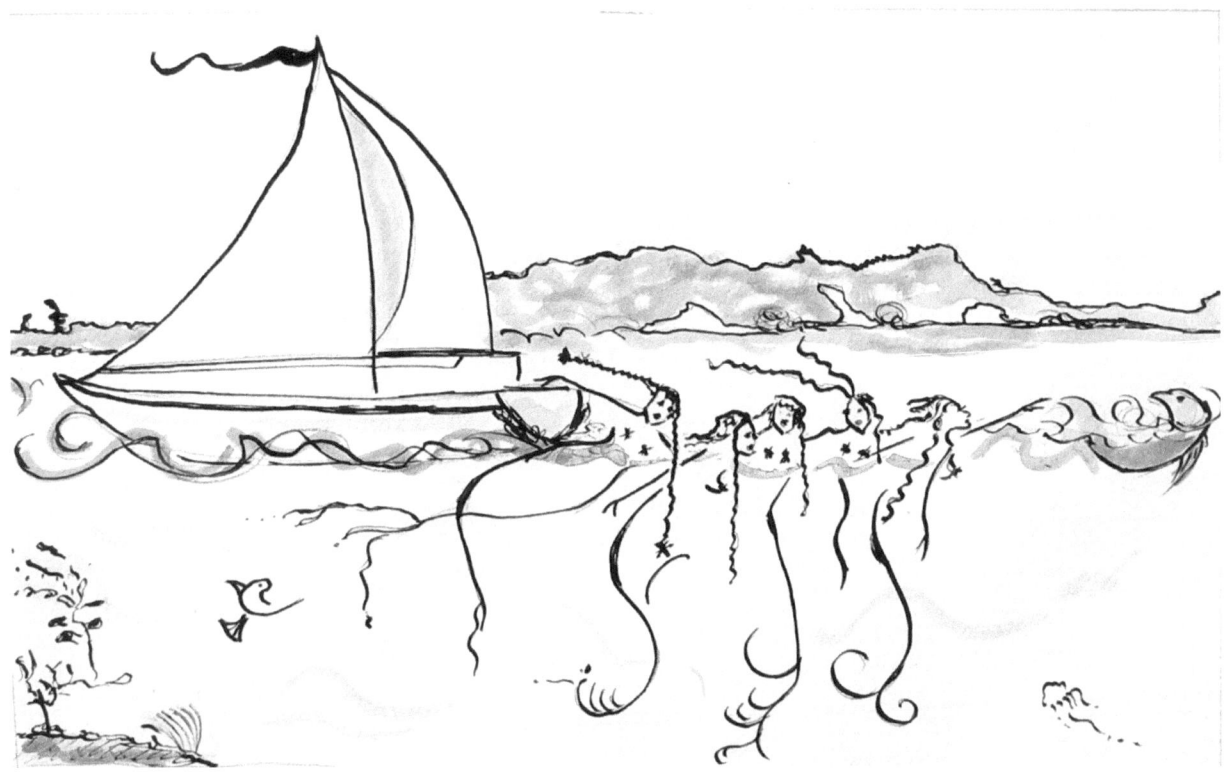

REBEKAH WILKINSON

www.rebekahwilkinson.com
rjwilkin@telus.net

Bio

Rebekah is a Fine Art graduate from the University of Guelph class of '95. In 2003, her artistic career began in Oakville, Ontario where she exhibited her acrylic paintings in the local libraries and restaurants. From there, her artist resume grew to include theatre set painting, mural painting and theatre set design for which she was nominated for "Best Set Design of a Comedy" in 2006 by the Association of Community Theatres of Ontario Central Region.

In December 2005, Rebekah was elected to the Oakville Arts Council Board and became the Chair of the Communications Sub-Committee for the Council. Rebekah was actively involved with the Arts Council until her move to Westbank, BC in the summer of 2007.

Since her move across Canada, Rebekah became involved with some of the local community art groups – Livessence and The Painter's Studio. Rebekah is currently the Exhibition Coordinator on the board of Livessence, a life-drawing group.

Rebekah exhibits her work with these community art groups and in local art fairs including Artwalk 2009. Her paintings can be seen at Raymond James, Kelowna BC, Urban Bliss Hair & Body Works and the Cove Lakeside Resort in Westbank, BC. In 2009 Rebekah showcased 3 solo shows at the Place des Arts, Coquitlam, BC, A Woodside Design Gallery, and the Kelowna Community Theatre, Kelowna, BC. She also had a display of her paintings at the 2009 Penticton Dream House Tour.

In 2010, Rebekah's landscape paintings will be showcased at Wine Valley Accents Gallery in Summerland. Also, Rebekah participated in the U8 Show at Sopa Fine Arts Gallery, Kelowna. And, Rebekah's newest opportunity involves the opening of Studio 113, a small artist coop of 4 artists working together in studio space at the Rotary Centre for the Arts, Kelowna, BC.

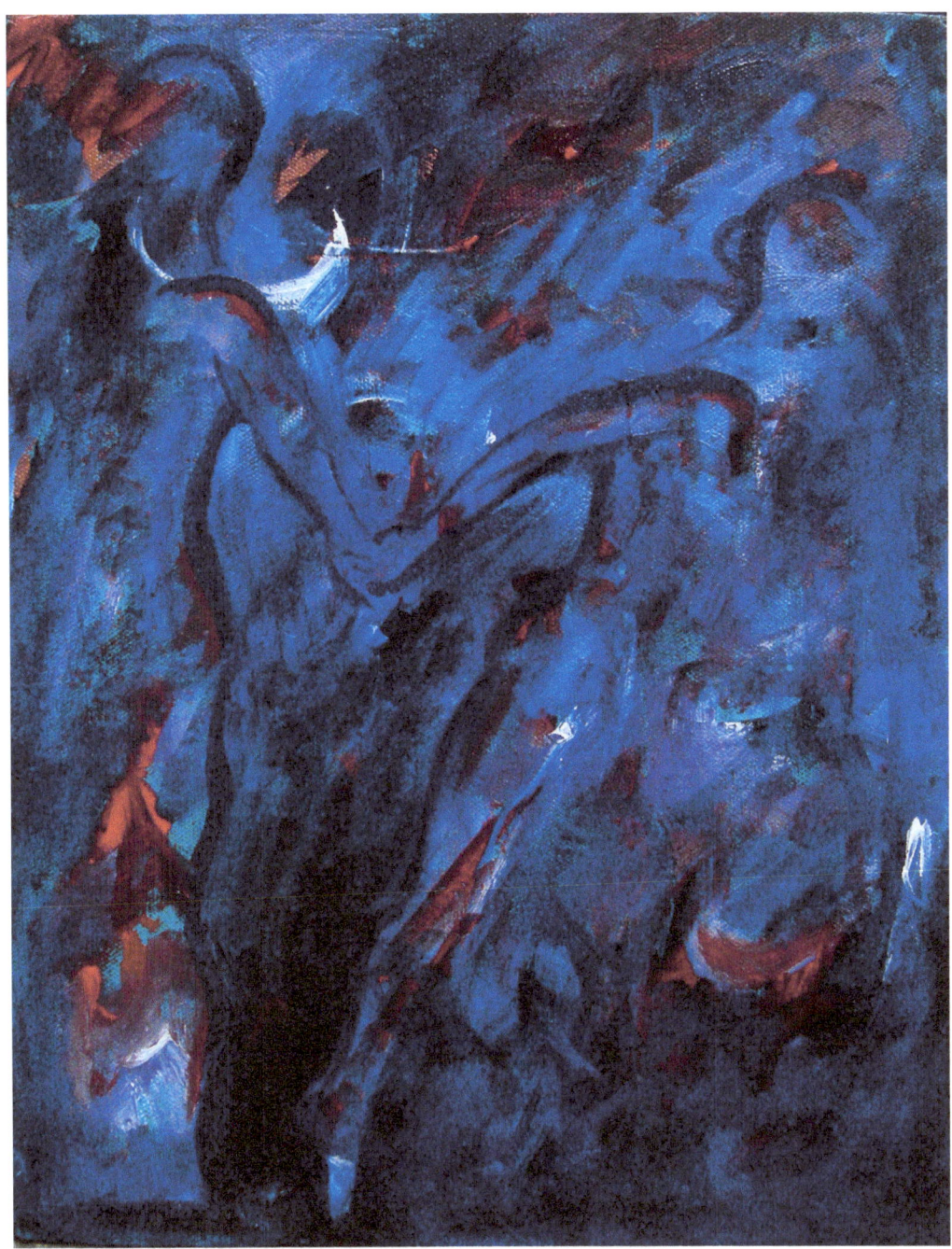

To Dance
Acrylic on canvas, 14x11

Let the brush strokes dance and the image will dance.

REBEKAH WILKINSON

Pas de deux
Acrylic on canvas, 14x11

Love and emotion in a ballet can often bring the audience to tears, but can this emotion come across in a painting? Music and movements create the feeling in a ballet, but can this be translated to a still? This is my personal artistic challenge. In addition, this particular call added the challenge of simplifying to a stick figure.

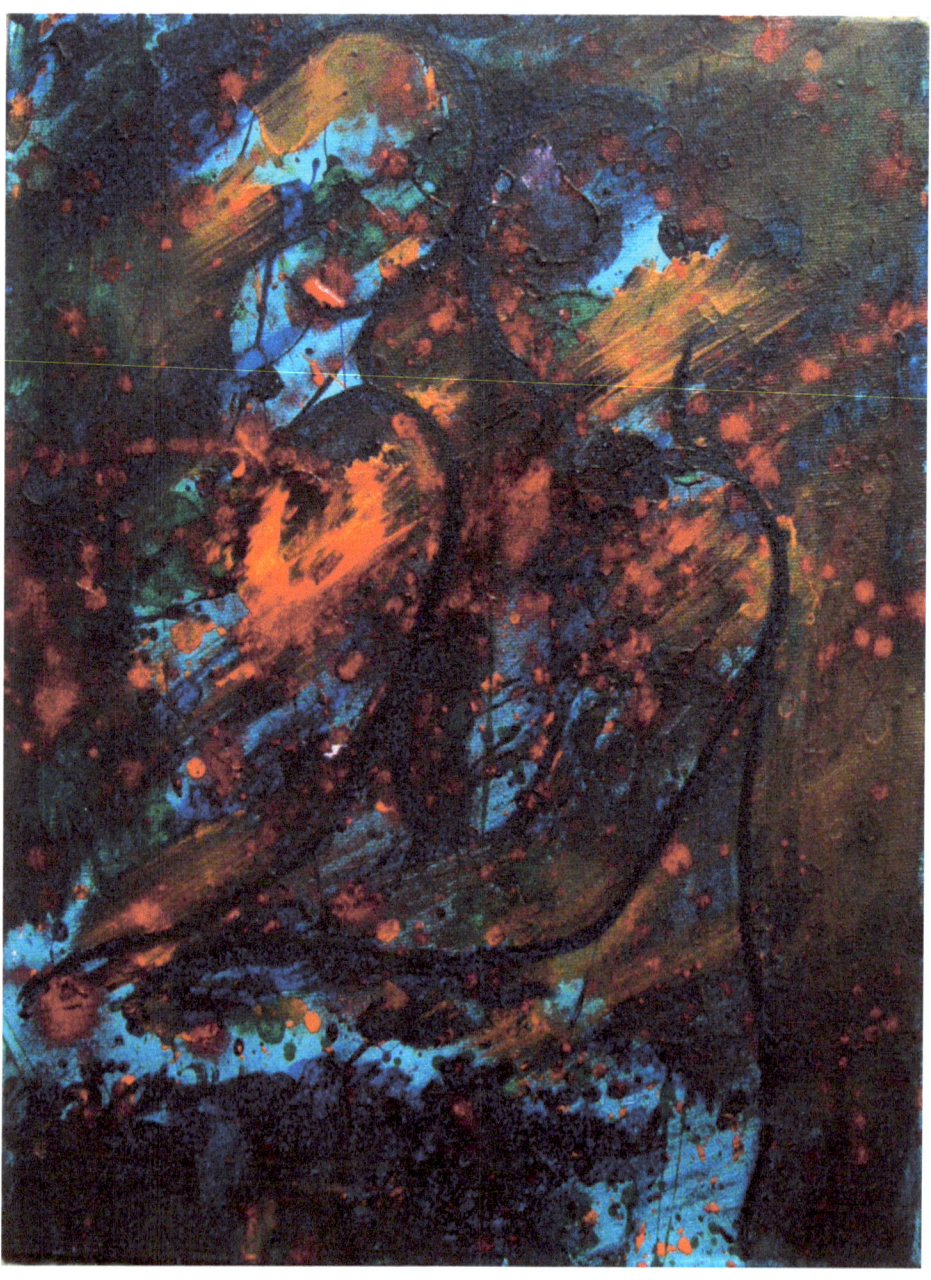

REBEKAH WILKINSON

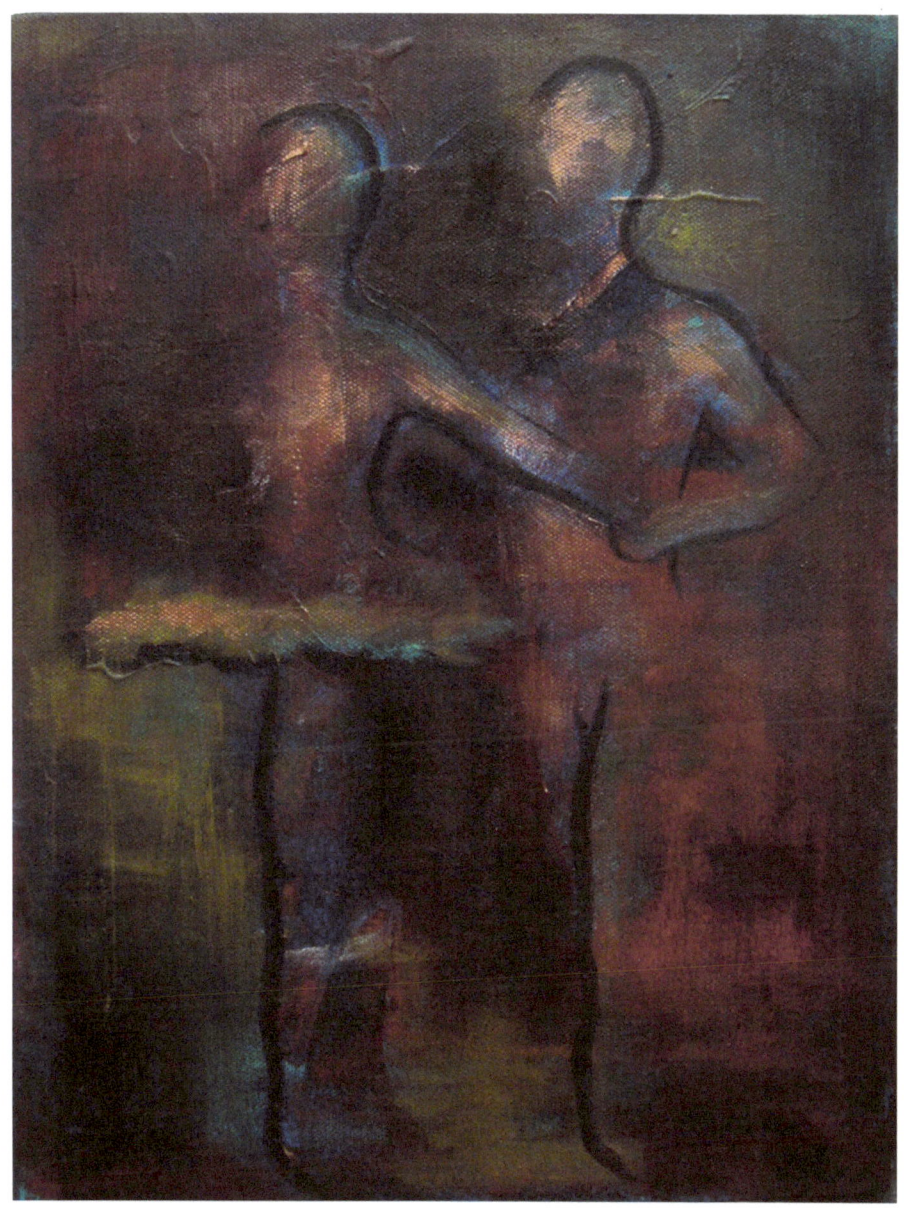

Everything is Turned Out
Acrylic on canvas, 14x11

Ballet is about precision and detail of the movement. Every step is highly refined right down to the legs being turned out into plié. Once the dancer masters the technical, only then can ballet become an avenue for artistic expression.

JULIA TROPS

www.juliatrops.com
julia@juliatrops.com

Bio

Being an artist is Julia's second career but first love. After a few failed attempts at University of Calgary, she left Calgary at the age of 22 to join the military. That seemed to be a drastic ticket out of Calgary, since, well, Calgary isn't really all that bad. Upon her retirement in 1997, after moving across Canada, living in almost each and every province as well as a peacekeeping tour of the Middle East, Julia returned to University at Lethbridge and received a BFA Great Distinction in Studio Arts.

 Since 2006, Julia's works have been published in art instruction manuals, the "Spirituality of" series by Woodlake Books, and she has written articles on the business of being an artist. In the past year, Julia has compiled the Okanagan Erotic Art Show Catalog and begun her own series of books based on her work and connections to her models, called "Julia's Model Series." The Livessence book "Simplicity in Mind" is another literary project.

Heavily involved in the arts community, the Okanagan Arts Awards, Okanagan Heritage Museum board director and a founder of Livessence and the Okanagan Erotic Art Show, Julia keeps pretty busy in her studio, having sold over 1000 works worldwide since 2004. Work may be obtained from Gallery Odin at Silverstar Ski Resort, Hambleton Galleries in Kelowna, Wine Country Accents in Summerland and/or the artist through the internet.

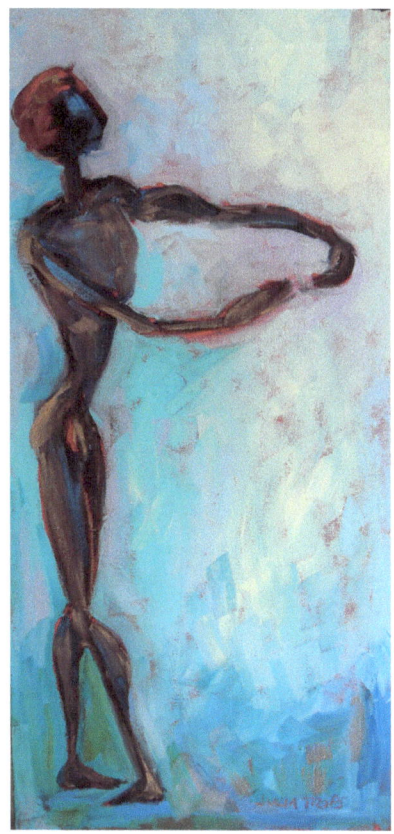

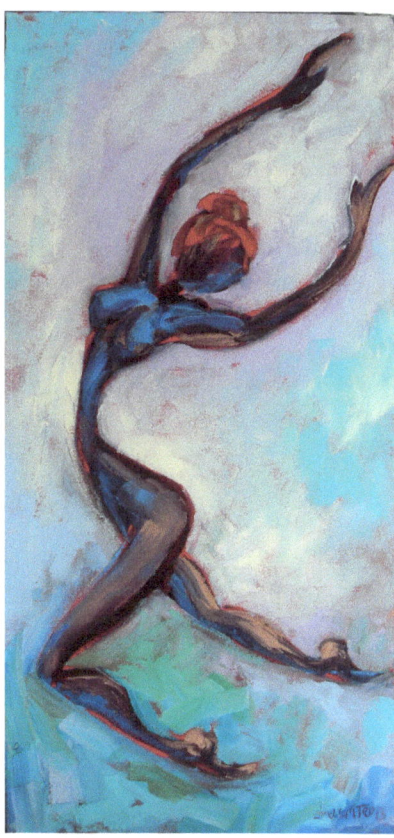

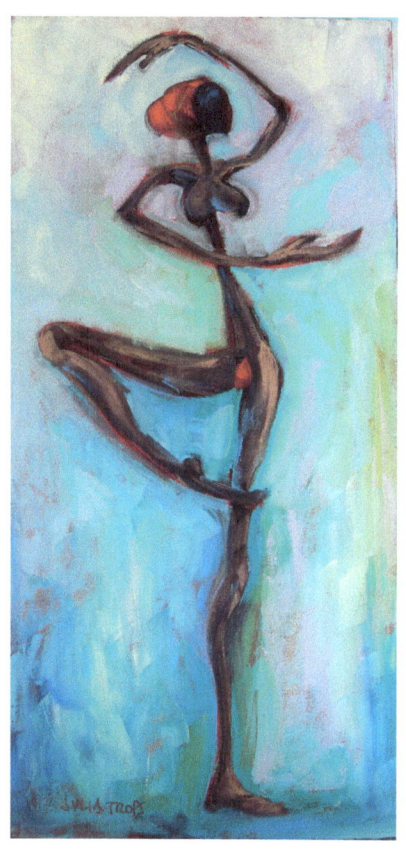

Circle of Life
Oil on canvas 20x10

Centre of Gravity
Oil on canvas 20x10

Balance
Oil on canvas 20x10

This particular series is one based on movement, colour and life.

Dance is one of the oldest forms of communication and is community based. It tells a story, entices one to action, or celebrates life. While lines do not exist in nature and are a construct of man, it is the one thing that I believe is the simplest form of communication.

JULIA TROPS

Light and Laughter 1
Oil on canvas, 24x24

Living in the Now, an existence which is reached during creative process, transforms all boundaries and our universe is limitless in the mind and heart and soul.

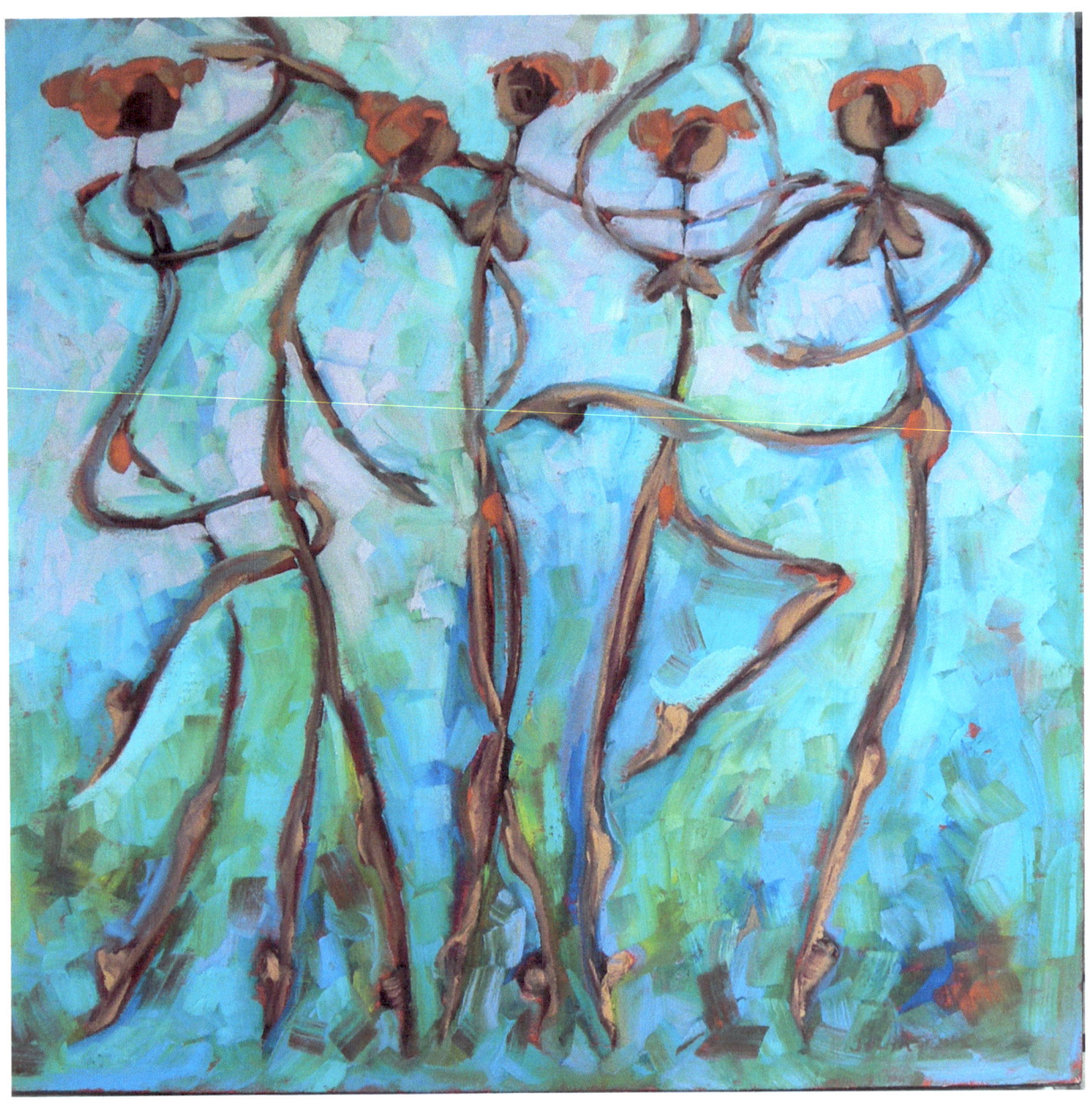

JULIA TROPS

Light and Laughter 2
Oil on canvas, 24x24

Description of the figure is limited to basic lines and simple curves but I believe that sometimes one can find all the freedom desired within a set of well defined self imposed rules. And being the author of one's rules, they can be changed at any time.

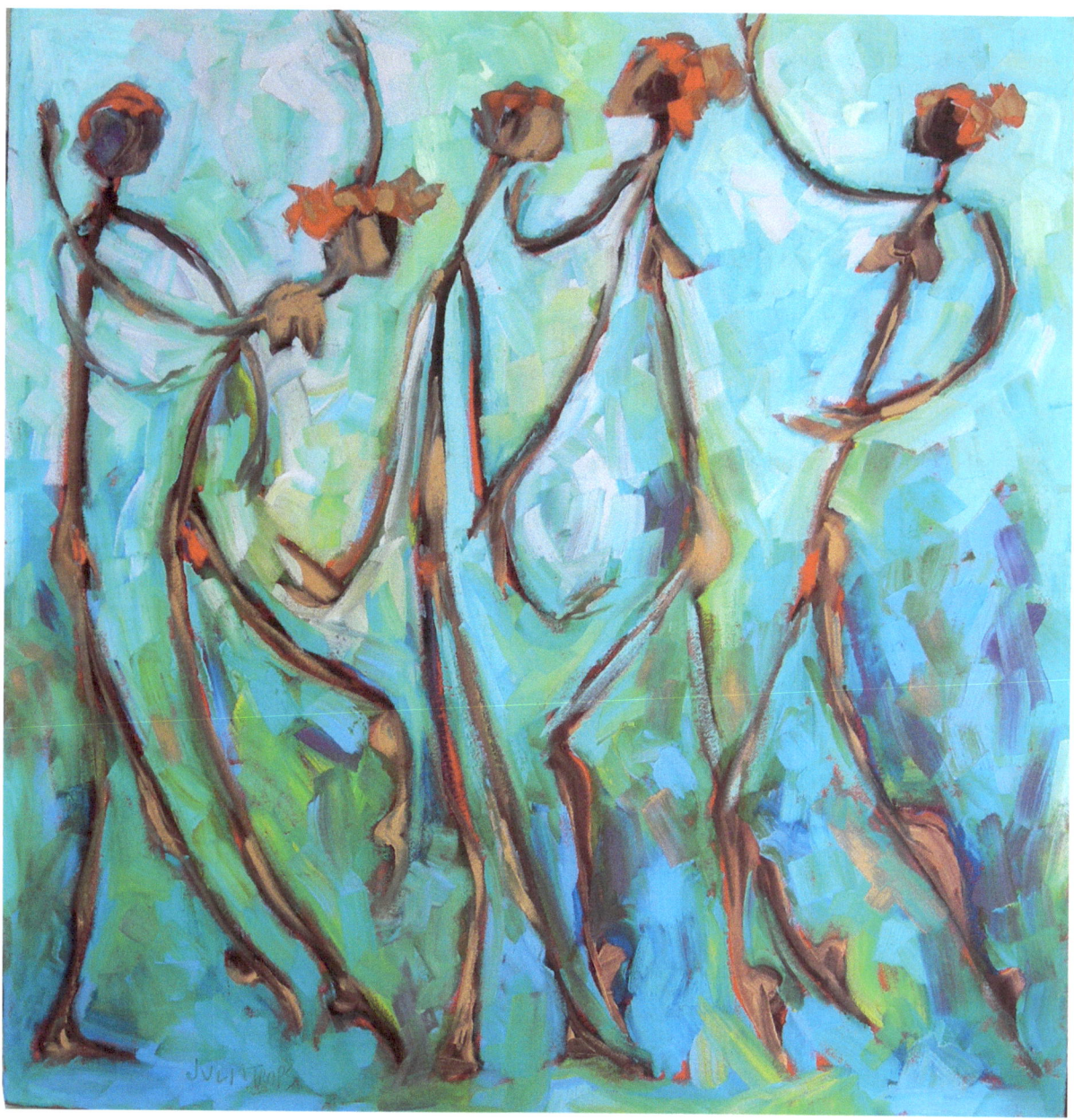

TINA SIDDIQUI

taeessuxmal@yahoo.com
http://creativepassion-tina.blogspot.com/
http://fineartamerica.com/profiles/tina-siddiqui.html

Bio

Born and raised in Pakistan, Tina travelled within the country and overseas with her diplomat father. Trained as a Graphic Designer, her artistic journey has been that of an explorer. Working in a variety of mediums, pastels are the medium of preference. Often enjoying an "explosion" of colours, Tina finds working with a limited palette equally thrilling. Light cascading over forms, natural or man made, is the driving force that compels her to paint as she strives to capture a specific moment in time. Her main interest is the multidimensional aspect of the human form, hence major part of her works are figures and faces.

Since 1976 she has exhibited in group and solo shows in United Kingdom, USA, Canada, Pakistan and Dubai and awarded for portraiture and abstract paintings, namely 2003 Opem International Portrait Competition in Toronto.

In 2004 Tina moved to Kelowna after a 13 year stay in Dubai. As an art educator for over 25 years, she was the recipient for the Art Educator Award for the Okanagan Arts Awards 2009. Teaching for her is exciting as she finds joy in her students' journey for self expression and she firmly believes it enriches her as an artist. Currently teaching a variety of classes in Kelowna, West Kelowna and Vernon.

TINA SIDDIQUI

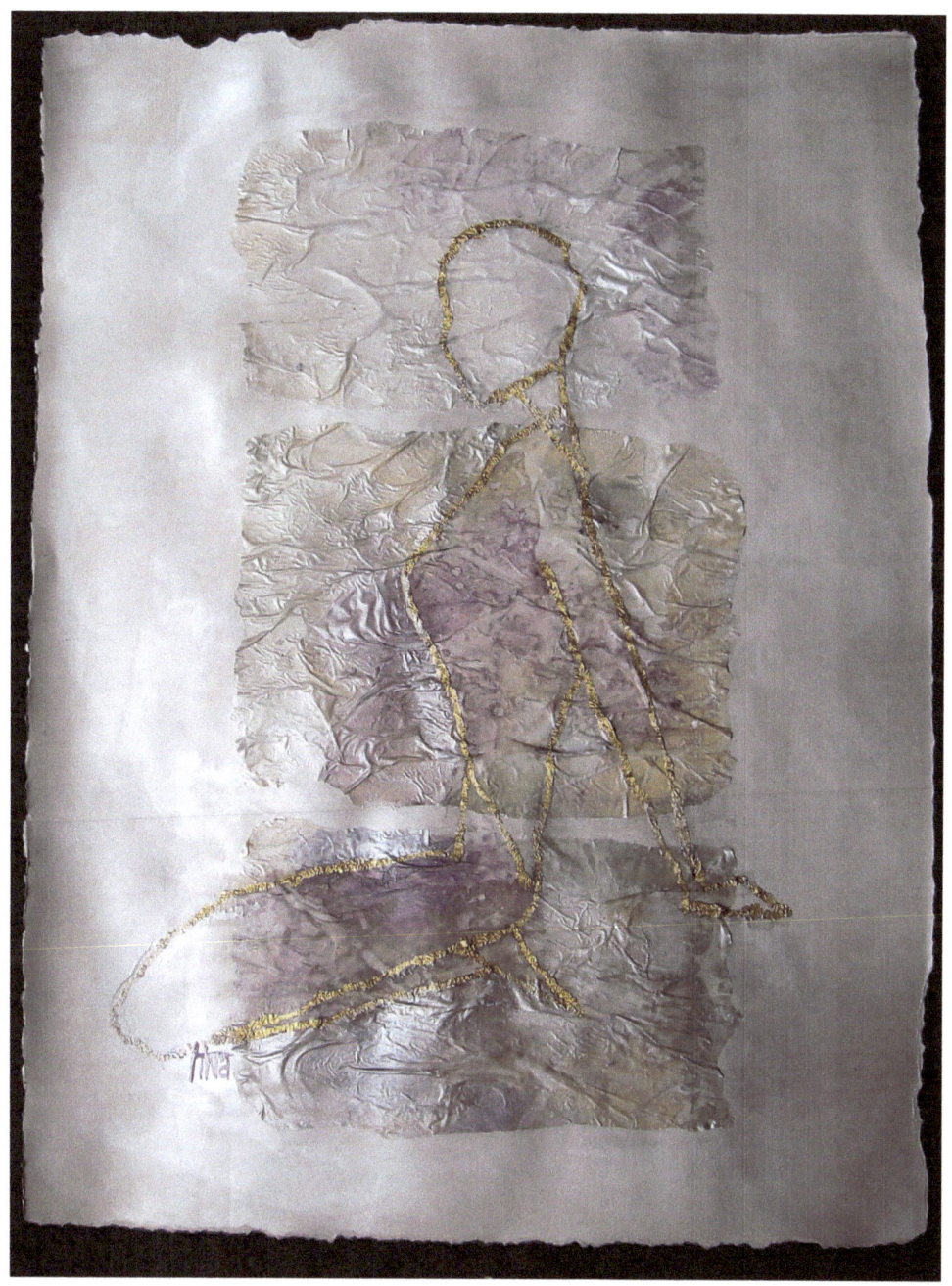

All that Glitters
Collage, 26x20

The simplicity of ancient Egyptian figures with strong lines is the source of inspiration for this collage. Figure is from one of my studies of Ballet Kelowna's dancer sitting on the floor as she waited for her turn. Palette is subdued, soft colours were used to convey the elegance and grace of the dancer.

TINA SIDDIQUI

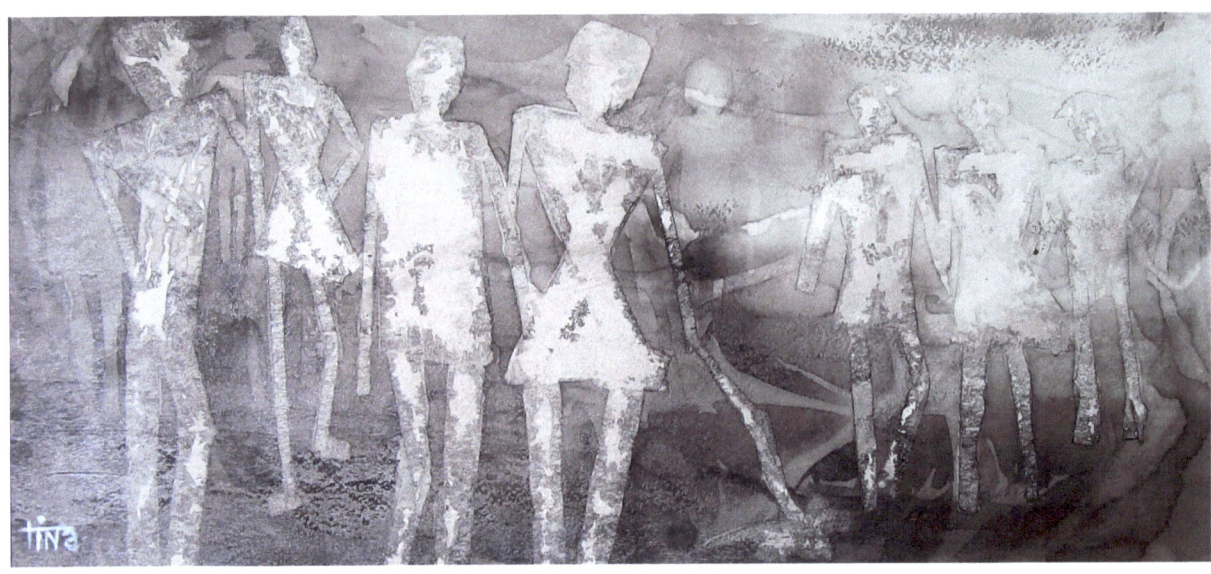

Family Stroll
Ink on paper, 25x11

As the much awaited summer spring/summer approached the Okanagan......the joy is seen all around...
parks, beaches, sidewalks, it is indeed a festive time of the year. I enjoyed creating the little canine family
member in the centre of this painting done in washes and layers of black ink.

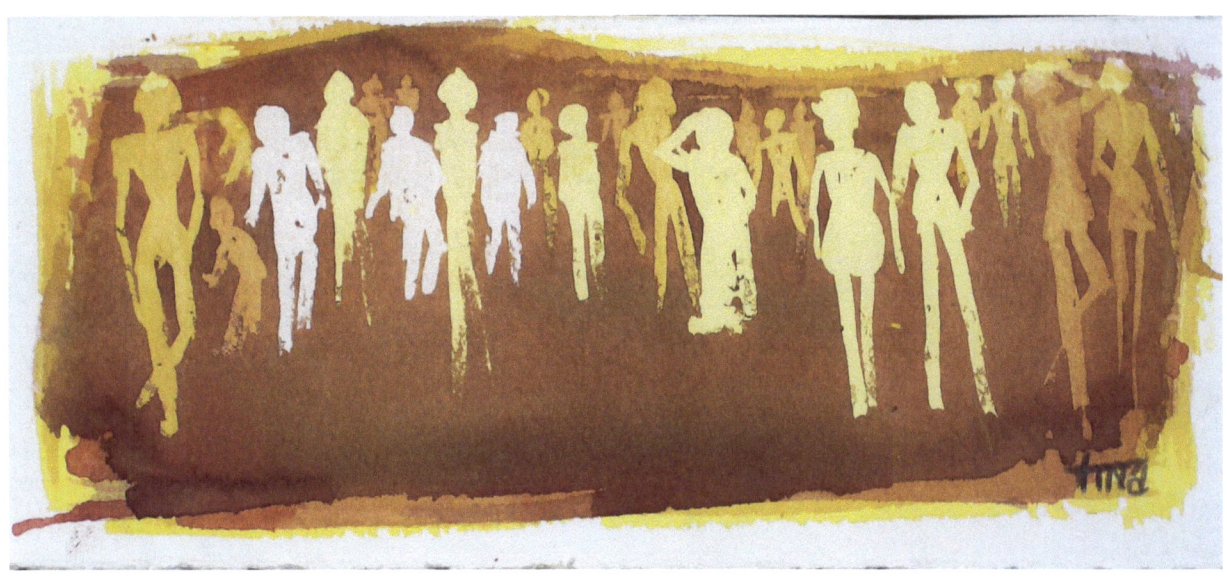

Evening Rush
Watercolours on paper, 9.5x4

Warm mono chromatic colours have always appealed to me, hence the palette for this work. Lingering memories of life in large metropolitan centres weave in and out of my imagination, I am so glad I moved out of that chaos. My tribute to those who have to deal with the evening rush after a long day's work.

TINA SIDDIQUI

In the Mist of Africa
Acrylics on canvas, 30x24

Lean physique of the Masai and other tribes of East Africa immediately came to my mind as I started to ponder on the call for "stick figures". Choice of colours is limited, trying to capture the grey greens of the region.

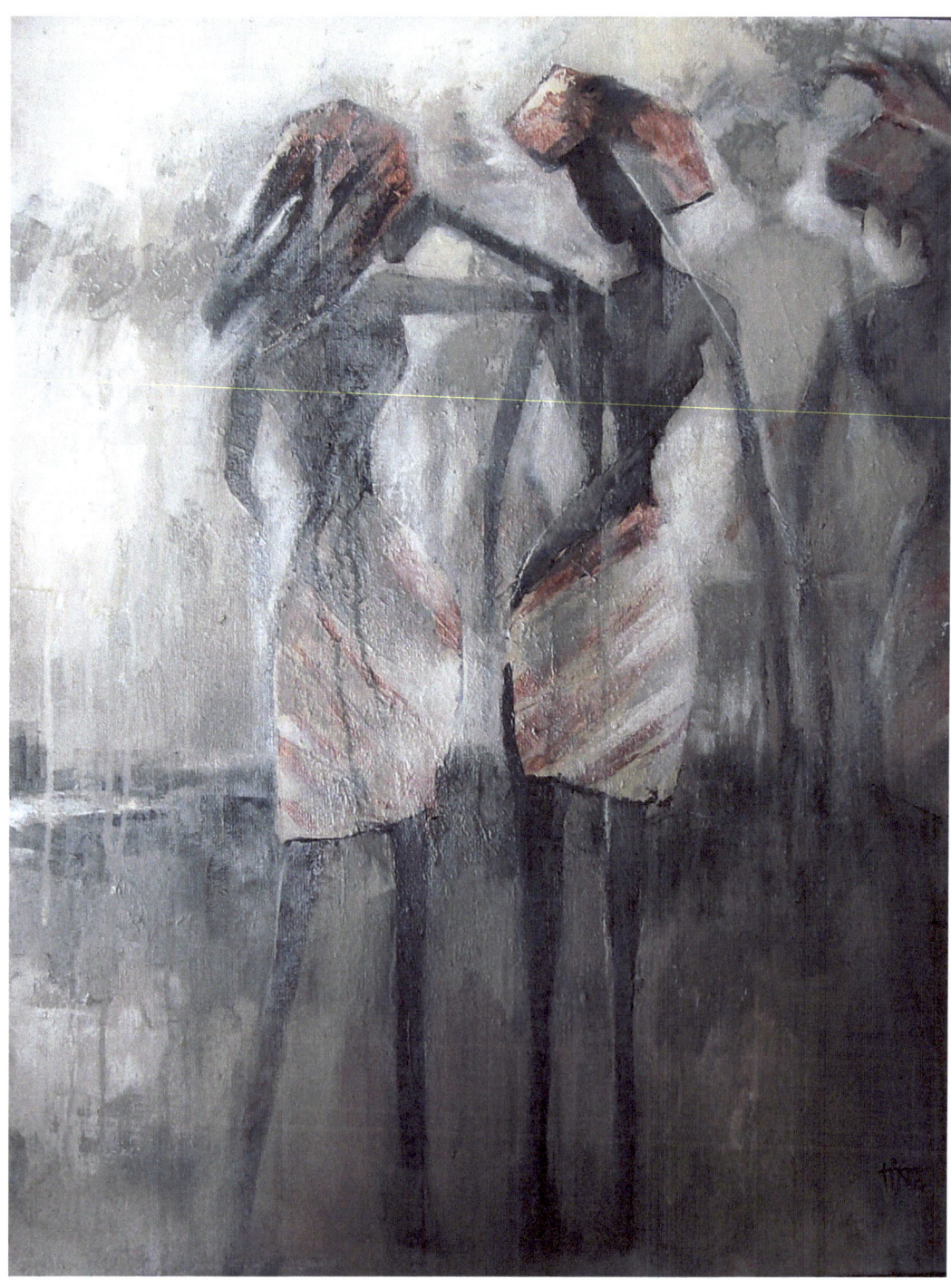

Swan Lake
Acrylics on canvas, 30x30

The experience of watching the dancers of Ballet Kelowna from behind the scenes was an awe inspiring experience for me. Their remarkable skills and hard work is what I tried to depict in this heavily textured painting. I enjoyed experimenting with the 2 colours used here.

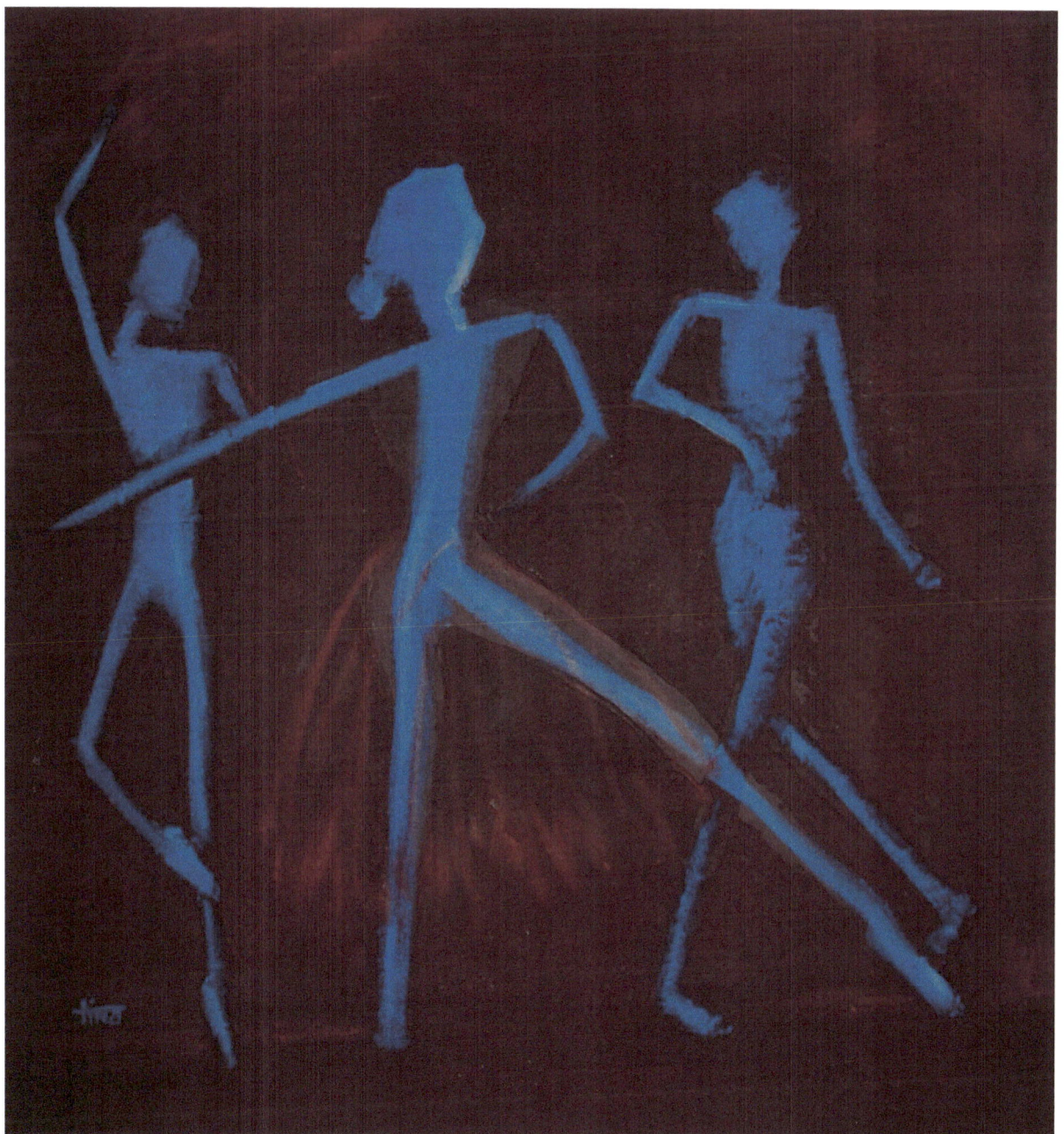

SIMPLE QUOTES

The simplest things give me ideas - Joan Miro

How difficult it is to be simple - Vincent Van Gogh

The most complex things are the simplest - Agni Celeste

Less is more. God is in the details - Mies van der Rohe

Silent and serene, forgetting words, bright clarity appears before you - Hongzhi Zhengjue

The art of art, the glory of expression and the sunshine of the light of letters, is simplicity - Walt Whitman

Simplicity is the final achievement. After one has played a vast quantity of notes and more notes, it is simplicity that emerges as the crowning reward of art - Frederic Chopin

Simplicity and repose are the qualities that measure the true value of any work of art - Frank Lloyd Wright

As I grew older, I realized that it was much better to insist on the genuine forms of nature, for simplicity is the greatest adornment of art - Albrecht Durer

Simplicity, carried to an extreme, becomes elegance - Jon Franklin

The ability to simplify means to eliminate the unnecessary so that the necessary may speak - Hans Hofmann

To see things simply is the hardest thing in the world - Charles Hawthorne

You can paint an entire painting with one stroke - Quang Ho

Never put more than two waves in a picture; it's fussy - Winslow Homer

Reduction! One wants to say more than nature and one makes the impossible mistake of wanting to say it with more means than she, instead of fewer - Paul Klee

With greater completeness and abstraction, I have attained a form filtered to its essentials - Henri Matisse

By painting a thing as simply as possible, you can get to the spirit of it. And then subject and artist reveal themselves to each other - Charles Movalli

Silence is one of the hardest arguments to refute - Josh Billings

DIANNE SCHNIEDERS

www.dianneschnieders.com
dschnieders@shaw.ca

Bio

Dianne majored in Art at the University of Calgary, Alberta and taught for 32 years,and as an Art Specialist for the last fifteen of those years. Her art training also includes numerous workshops. Since 2002 she has been able to devote herself full-time to her art and developing her skills. She works in various media, specializing in water media,graphite,ink and charcoal.

In searching for her own voice she has been influenced by Chinese brush technique and discovered pouring watercolor which takes advantage of this medium's luminosity. She likes to work with a limited palette. Combined with her skill in rendering images,she captures expression and mood in her paintings. She has a fine sense of balance in her work. She draws on a lifetime of experience with dogs and horses but does not limit herself to just these subjects. Wherever her imagination takes her is explored.

Dianne has exhibited her work in Western Canada and the U.S. Her work has been well received in Colorado. She is an active member of the Federation of Canadian Artists and Livessence, a life drawing association.

Her work hangs in many private and corporate collections.

DIANNE SCHNIEDERS

After Raphael
Mixed media on paper, 21x30

It intrigued me that even the best artists we know, like the Renaissance painter, Raphael, had to begin with a design so I abstracted one of his famous paintings to stick figures to show the beautiful sweep of curves he envisioned. This piece follows a long tradition of copying the Masters to practise technique.

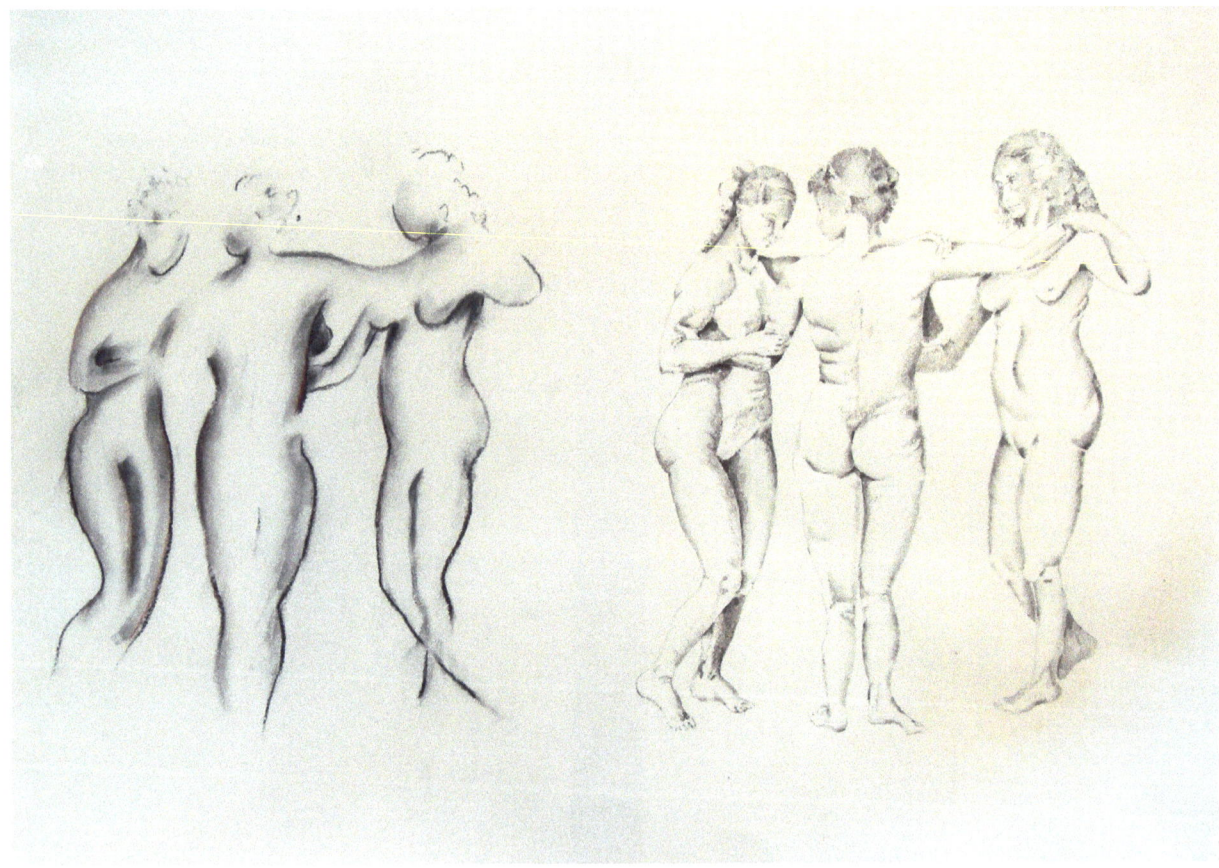

Harlequin
Watercolour on paper, 14x28

This was an interesting challenge-to create pieces for "Stick Figures". I was intrigued by the notion that we all started at the same place with art-our first attempts at depicting the figure- then built on it through time, practice and education, to where we are in our art today. Harlequin depicts that progression.

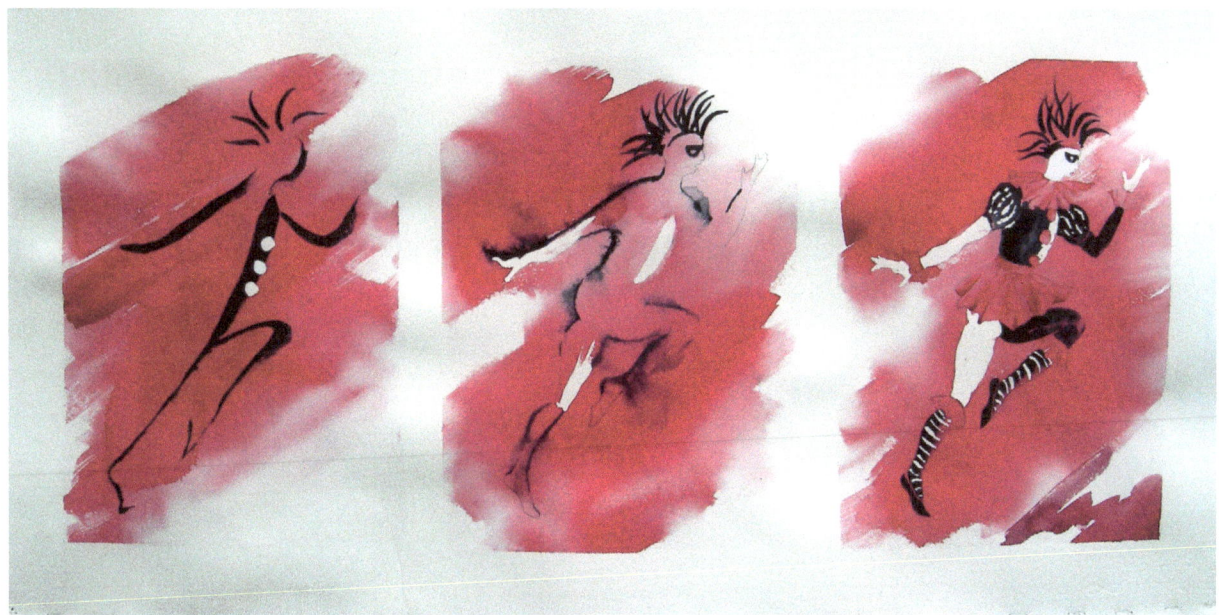

TINA SCHNELLERT

tschnellert@telus.net

Bio

Tina was born in California and later moved to Canada. Formally trained in commercial art, Tina has also pursued her education in fine art by attending numerous accomplished artist's workshops over the years. She has painted and showed with 'The Kelowna Watercolor Guild' and 'The Livessence Society for Figurative Artists'. Tina listens for the muse and lives in a mode of exploration.

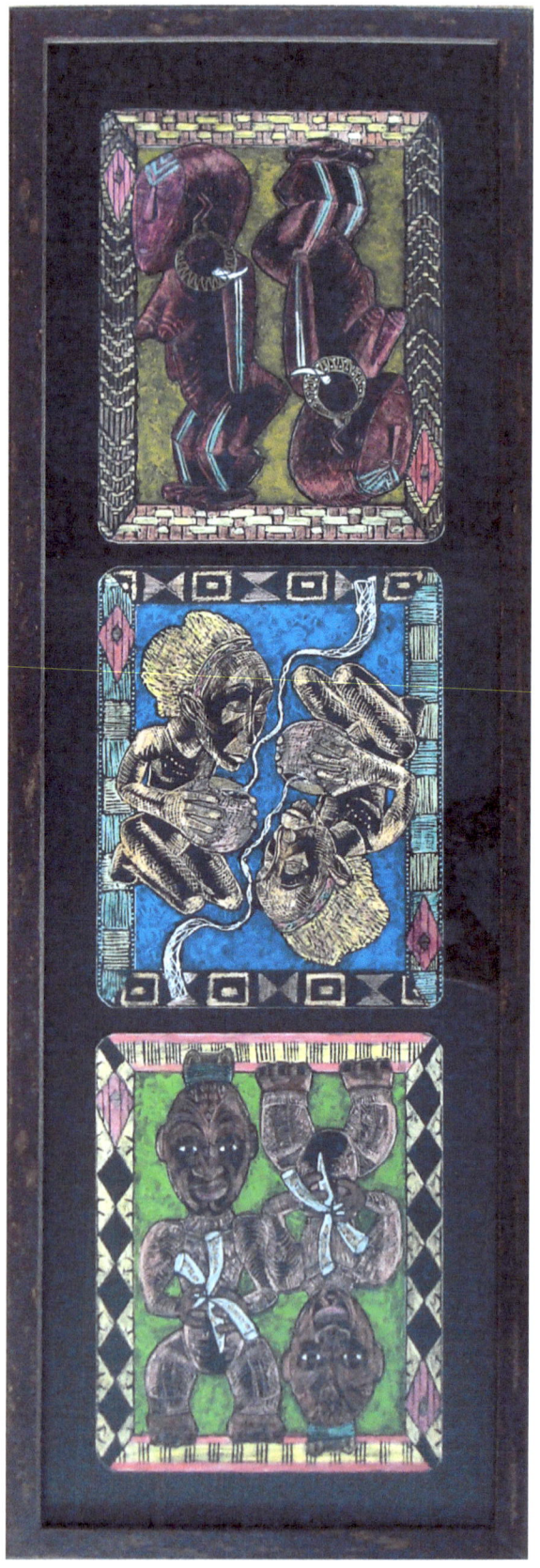

Queen, Jack, King
Mixed media on scratch board, 14x41.5

Viewers marvel at an artists ability to produce a creative piece but it is truly a primitive instinct. From the ancient outlined shape of a hand on a dark cave wall to tribal figures crudely carved from sticks - we perceive that there has been an insistent creative force. The three carved icons in this piece where produced to urge contemplation of our need for security through power and spirituality and our desire to produce art to compensate for our transitory nature.

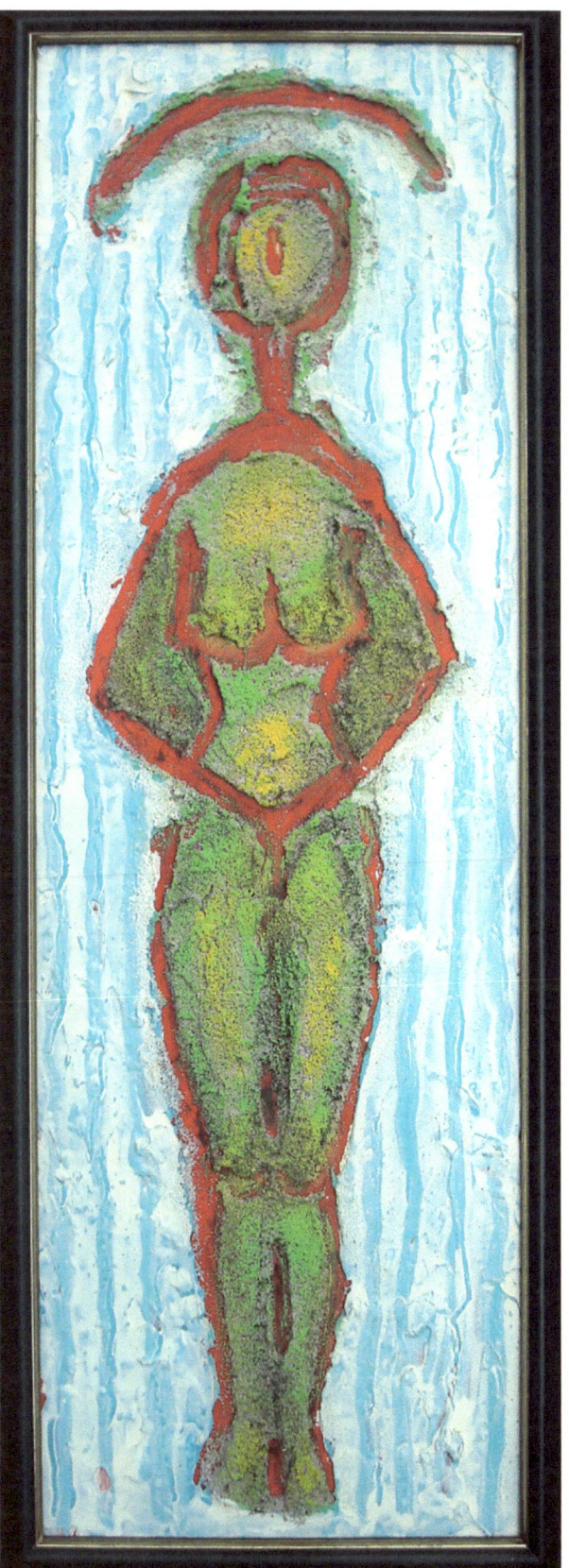

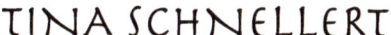
TINA SCHNELLERT

Reliquary Guardian
Mixed media on board, 8x24

Reliquary figures, often found in early African art, were guardians of enshrined sacred relics. This simplified outline line of a woman, with hands in prayer position in front of the reproductive organs, eludes to the sacrosanctity and responsibility that comes with the ability to bring forth life.

RALF ROHRLACK

ralf@greystokedesign.com

<u>Bio</u>

Ralf Rohrlack was born in Berlin, Germany and immigrated with the family to Alberta, Canada in 1954. The self-taught artist developed his artistic skills working for leading graphic and architectural design corporations. His enjoyment of the outdoors and sports became the subject of many of his paintings. The vastness of the Prairies and the grandeur of the Canadian Rockies are reflected in much of his art. He and his wife moved to the Okanagan in 1975. His involvement the art community included exhibits at wineries and the Kelowna Art Gallery. Having lived in Spain and Mexico broadened his subject matter. Joining a figurative art group allowed for the inclusion of people and their activities.

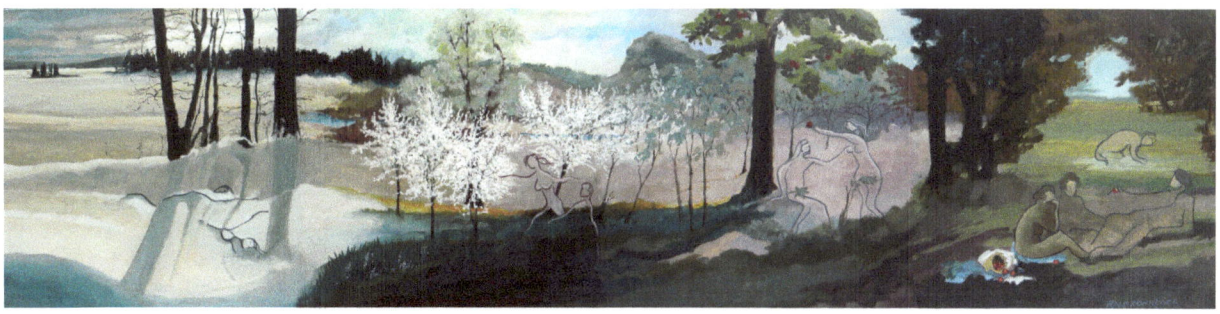

Evolution of the Stick Figure
Acrylic on canvas, 12x48

Painting "Stick Figures was the last thing on my artistic horizon. Very early one morning, though, ideas started to play with my head. A theme based on Adam and Eve and Darwin's Theory of Evolution became the subject of the "Stick Figure". As I kept developing the theme Vivaldi's classic "The Four Seasons" came to mind for the scenes in the order of Carole Kings lyrics "… Winter, Spring, Summer or Fall…" in the song "You've got a Friend". These became the four panels: "The Evolution of the Stick Figure".

RALF ROHRLACK

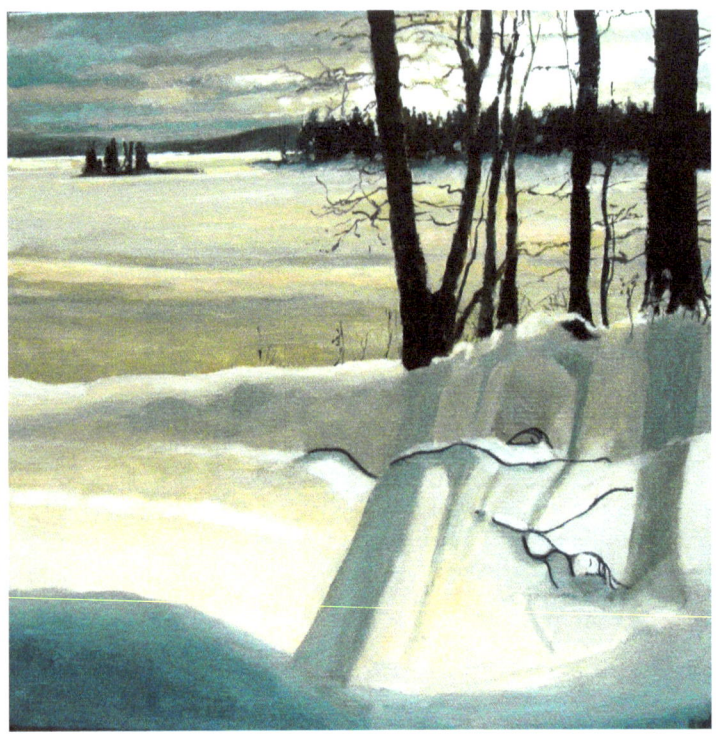

The Evolution of the Stick Figure
(close ups)

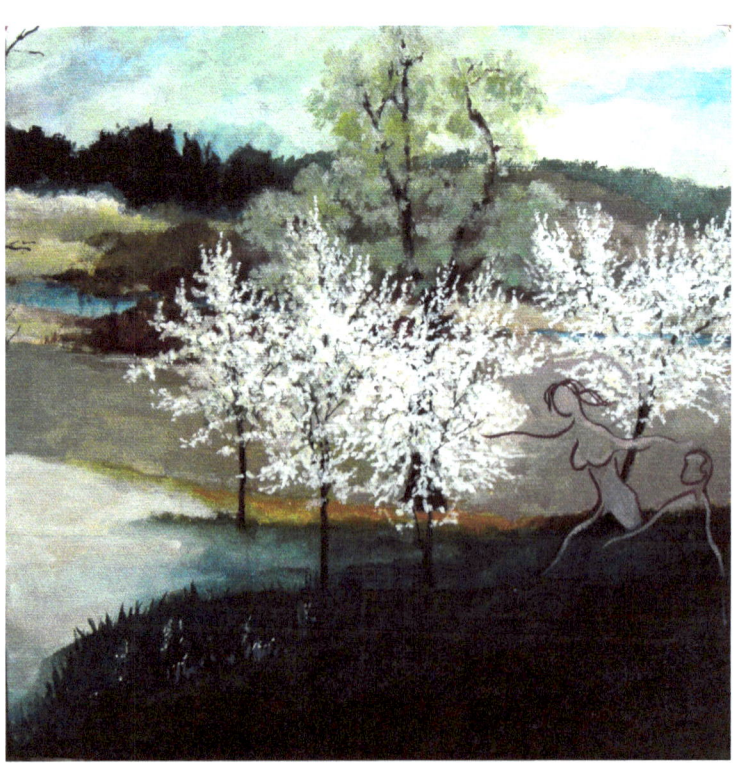

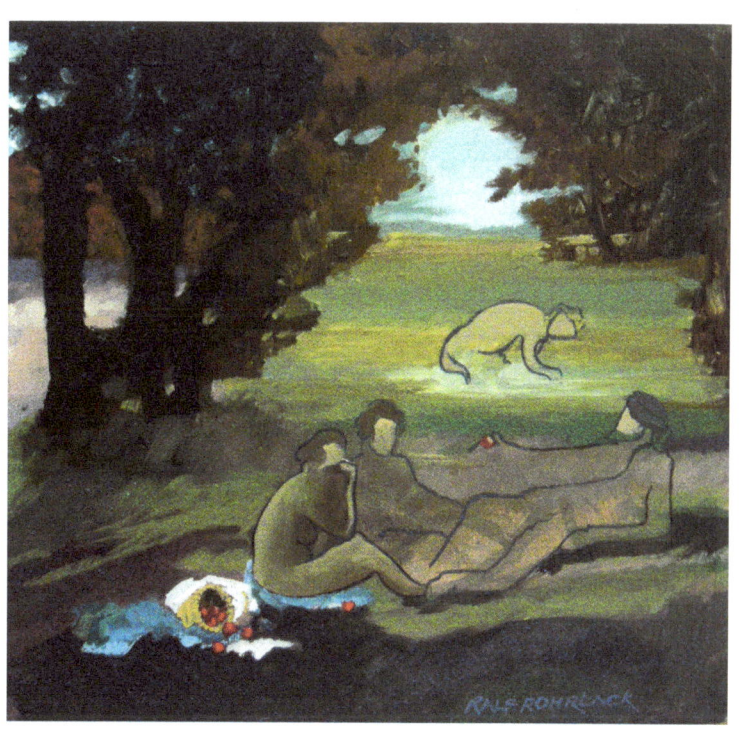

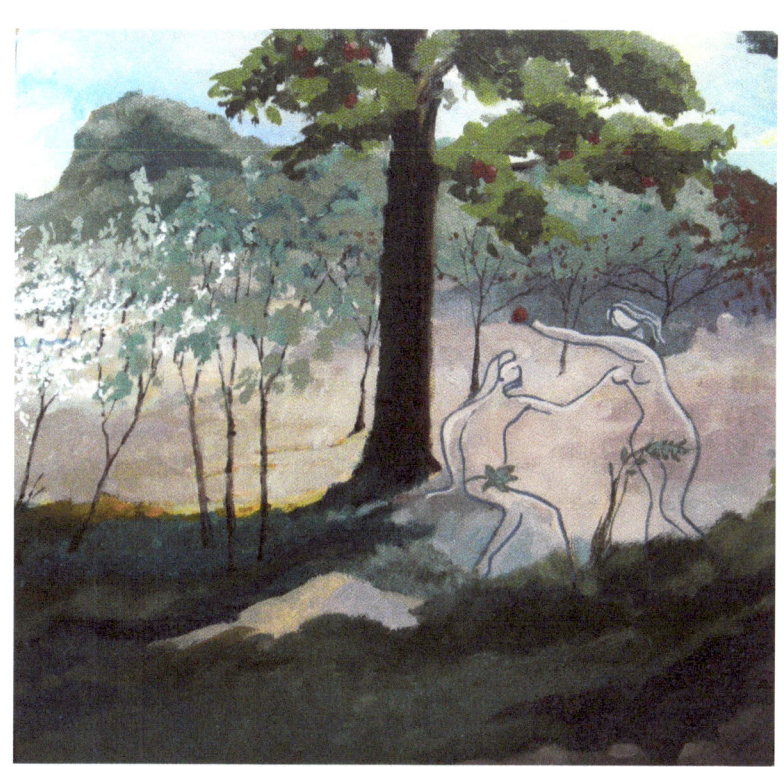

AMY BURKARD

www.amybydesign.com
amybgirl@gmail.com

Bio

Amy Burkard is a Kelowna based visual artist who has been presenting work professionally for over 10 years. Originally from Courtenay, BC, Amy realized in her mid 20's that being a professional artist would be the best career she could envision. After completing her BFA at Emily Carr University of Art + Design in 2003 her creative voice as Canadian female artist emerged. Guided by material curiosity, she continues to discover her dream.

Currently her practice involves what she has termed, "open to experiment." This definition describes her broad variety of interests, which include: clay, fiber, printmaking, marbling, painting, life drawing, and even digital printing. She states that her "artistic borders are open", allowing a lot of room for experimentation and creative growth.

Stick Figures show theme presented an interesting premise to create a theme around, at first I thought it would be too basic and leave me unfulfilled just drawing something so simple as a stick figure. Although, soon after I began to further explore the idea I realized it had the capacity to be as complex as I wanted. In the end I found it a welcome challenge that pushed me and allowed me widen the way I perceive artistic value.

Movement
Pencil on paper, 14x11

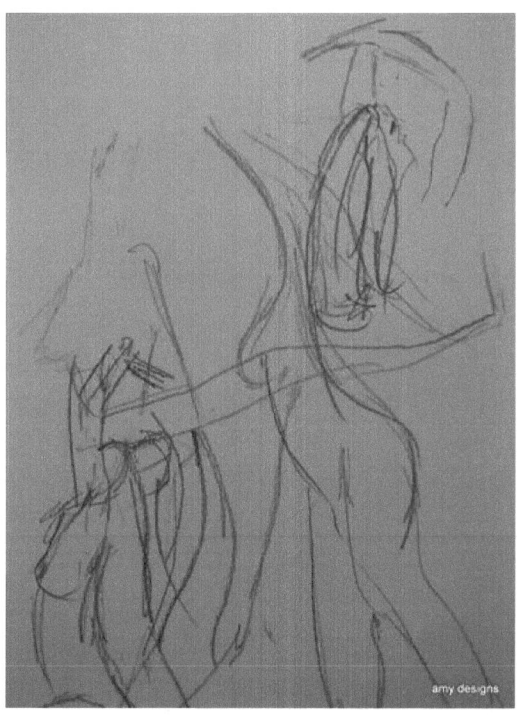

The Diver
Oil stick on paper 14x11

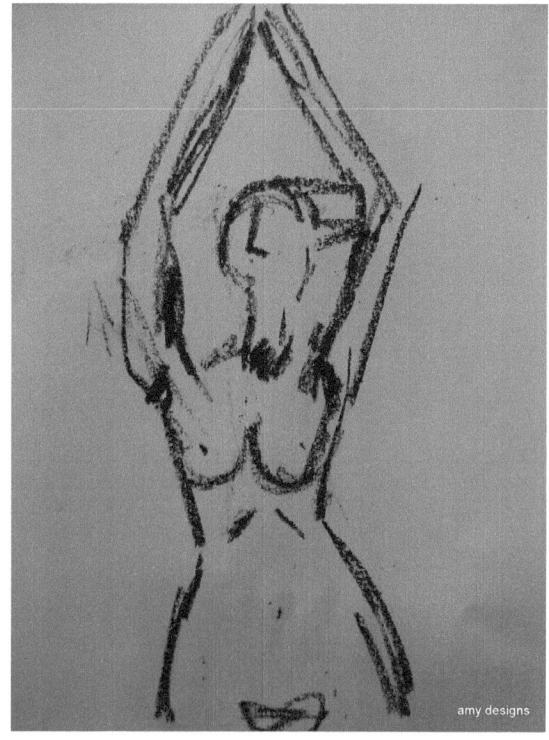

AMY BURKARD

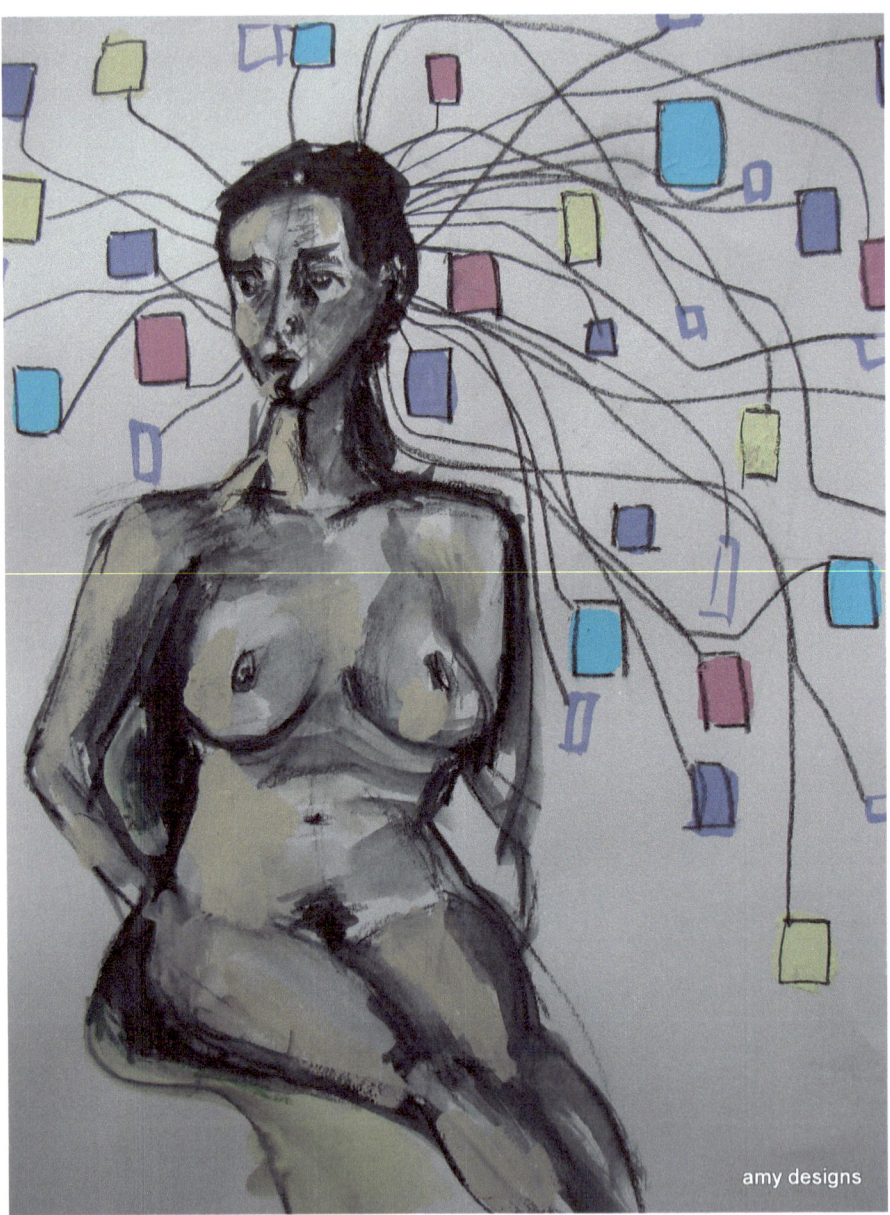

Compartmentalizing Thoughts
Watercolour pencil & gouache on paper, 14x11

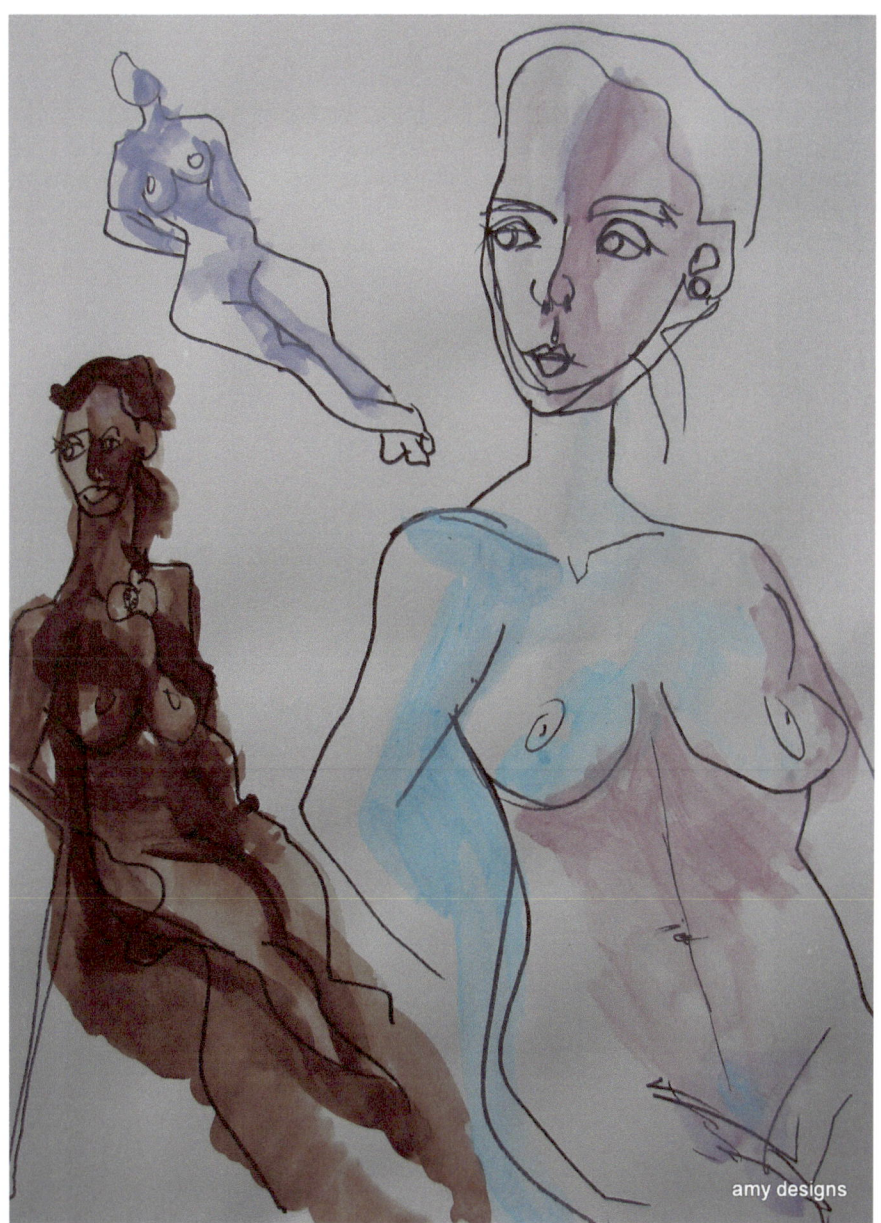

amy designs

The Gaze
Marker & gouache on paper 14x11

SANDRA BRADSHAW

www.sandrabradshaw.com
sbradshaw@telus.net

Bio

Sandra Bradshaw is a self-taught artist that has lived and worked in the Okanagan for the past 10 years. Although she makes the occasional foray into other areas she always returns to the body as her favorite subject. "Movement is dynamic and the body is a magnificent vehicle for that movement. My professional work as a somatic practitioner has given me the opportunity to immerse myself in human movement and movement potential on a daily basis which has informed my art.

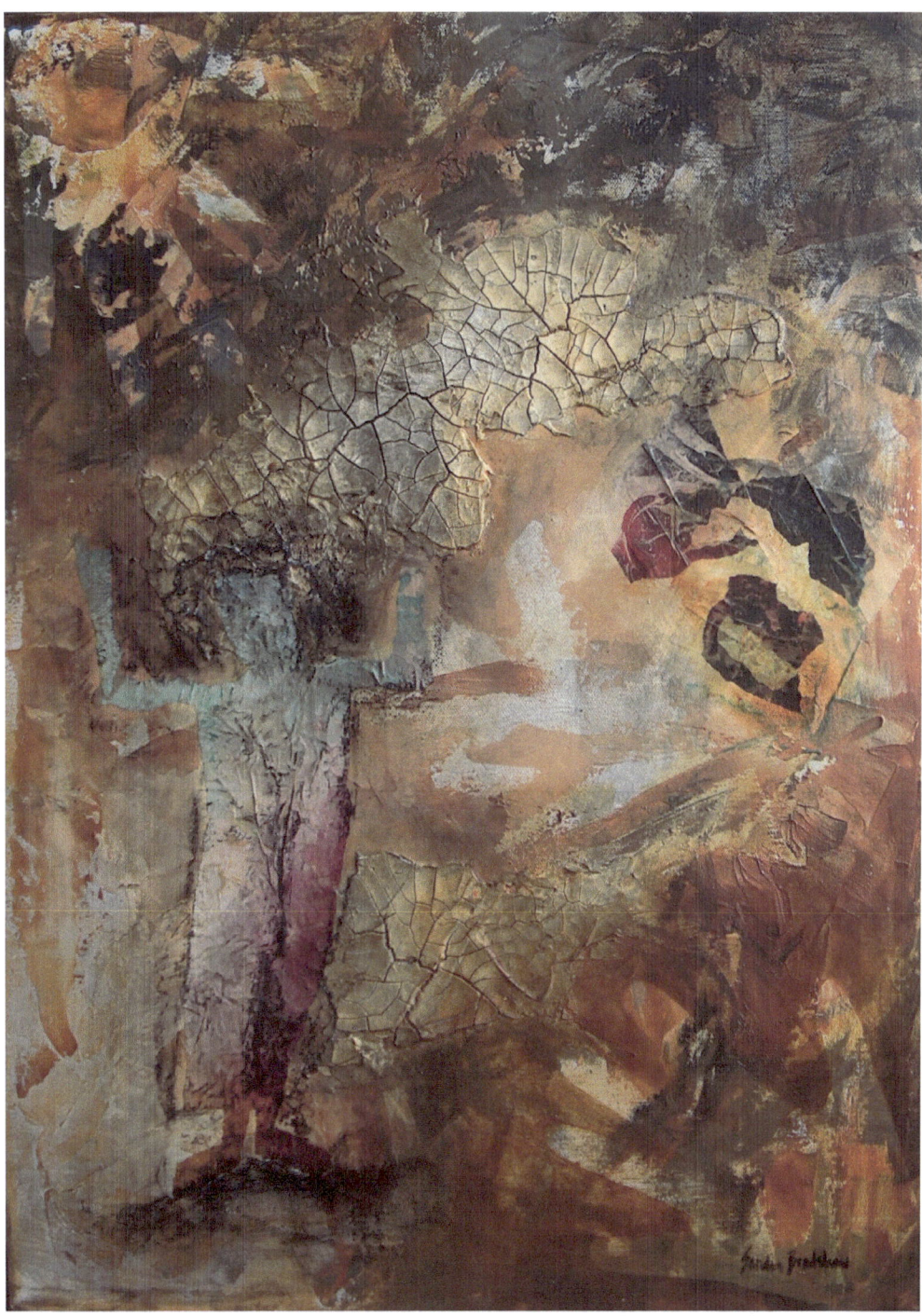

Corn Mother
Mixed media 23x18

Corn Mother, the Goddess of fertility and life, guardian of all growing and blooming things, and Goddess of death and rebirth sacrifices herself at the harvest, only to be reborn in the spring. I open myself to receive Corn Mother's gifts.

SANDRA BRADSHAW

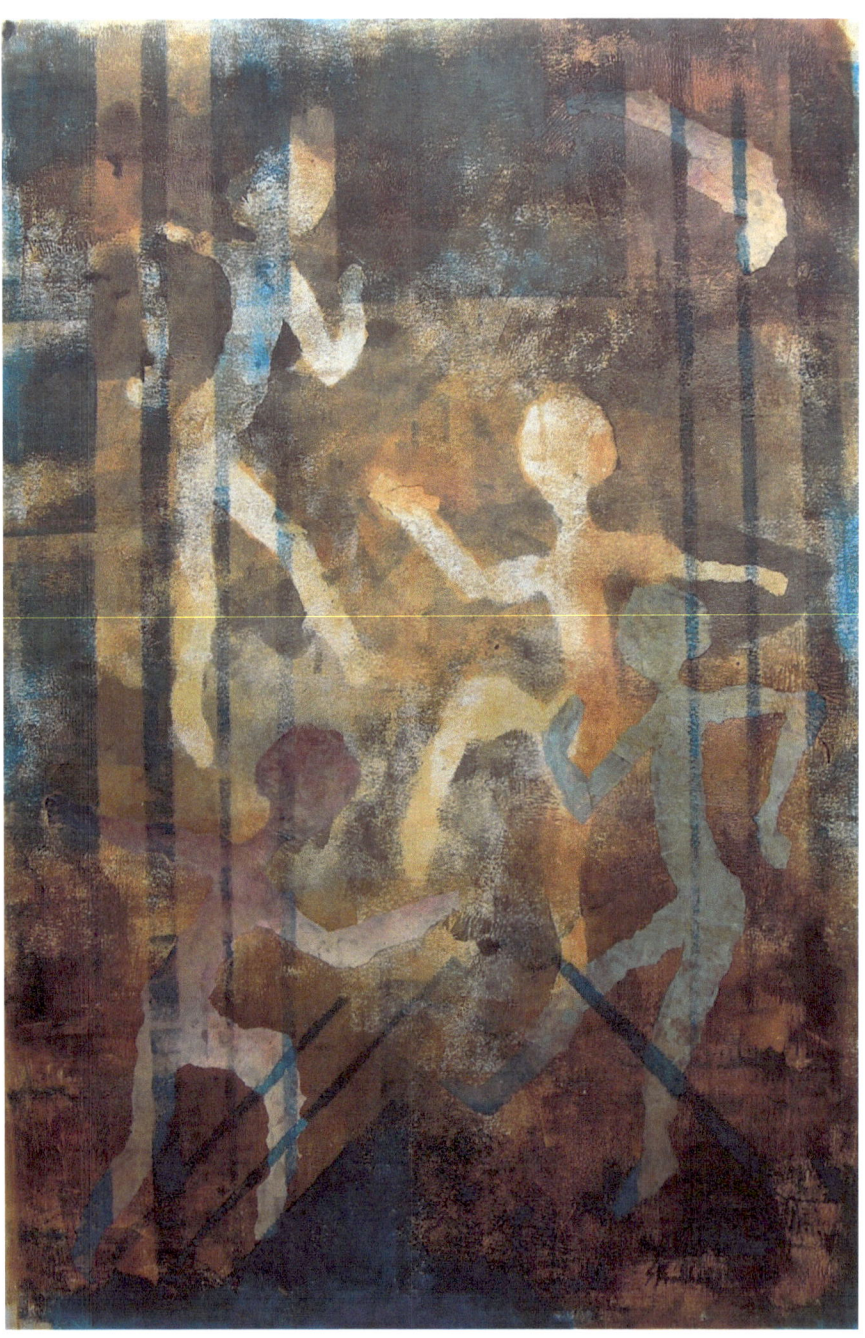

Shadow Dancers
Mixed media, 21.5x14.5

The images in this piece are shadow forms that dance in my mind. Illusive and ephemeral, they disappear when I try to capture them on paper. Their forms are not fully fleshed but rather stick figures that will only develop further if I allow them to dance.

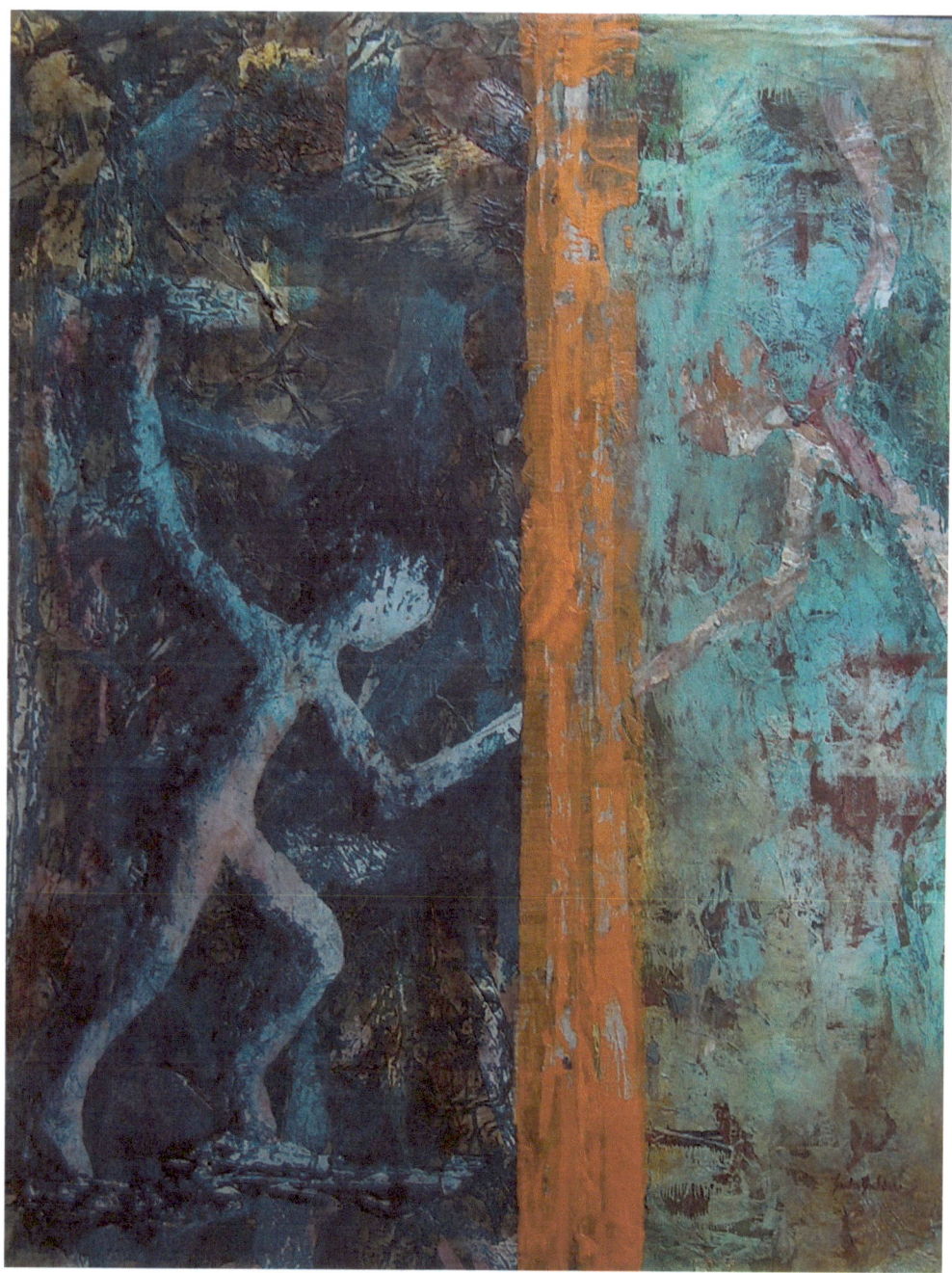

How Do I Get There From Here?
Mixed media, 36x24

What is the function of art? For me it's the ability to express something in a way that's not possible with words. In this piece, inner tension and frustration were expressed, the question asked and the viewer is now left to find her own answer.

IN CONCLUSION

The exhibition involving Stick Figures, "Simplicity in Mind" was a challenge for our drawing members and an ambitious project for the Society. I would say about half of our members are professional artists, making a living from their work, and the other half, those who just like to come and draw and enjoy the camaraderie and challenge the model presents each week. These are our artists.

This year, 2010, we have four exhibitions that are running fairly close together, with maybe two or three weeks apart. Sometimes that is just the way it works out. This created a challenge for our Exhibitions Chairman Rebekah Wilkinson to organize and facilitate these four exhibitions with approximately 35 members of varying degrees of ability. The goal of all our exhibitions is to nudge our members to push themselves just a little bit outside of their comfort zone, regardless of whether a full time or part time artist. I think we succeeded with this exhibition, in that we returned to the roots of creation, that of the simple line, something we learned about as children.

Interestingly, these simple lines created a bit of a consternation with our members. Should they keep the lines straight? How straight was too straight, how much detail can you give and how much information is really enough? What we have done, in essence (excuse the pun), is to expose our members to a form of Minimalism.

Minimalism in visual art came into "fashion" in the 1960s with such artists as Donald Judd, John McLaughlin, Agnes Martin, Dan Flavin, Robert Morris, Anne Truitt, and Frank Stella. While these artists pared down their paintings and sculptures to what there was on the surface or in the space, our artists worked on using line as a metaphor, a description for deeper meaning. They focused more on the idea of the primitive cultures going back to the beginning of time.

Simplicity has always been underestimated. Consider the expressions of the caveman, or the drawings and paintings of ancient civilizations; they tell stories and describe honour and success and defeat. We continue to speak in awe of their works but these people were not educated in post secondary or graduate schools, they relied on simple expression to communicate their thoughts, feelings and beliefs.

Lines can be evocative of life, living and dying. Lines can celebrate or condemn, depending on weight or movement. They prove you don't need to be a scholar to draw.

In the history of art, whether ancient Egyptian, African primitive, Australian, American or Canadian Aboriginals, regardless of their origin or homeland, their sources were the same. That of honour of the land, honour of the family, honour of the community, honour of their deities. Spirituality and art have always been linked, and in ancient times, it was simplicity creating the vehicle for impressions and worship enhanced by the person's own views and beliefs.

I daresay that many of our submitting artists did have fun with the project (after they were done!) and many of our artists did consider submitting. Some of their comments follow this text.

The book project came about because we plan on submitting these works to public galleries. It's an easy way to show a Society portfolio in a concise and professional manner. The goal of the exhibition is to engage the public, and help them understand that the artistic rendering of the human form is not all that elusive or unobtainable. One can draw in any manner, and it is that expression or goal that determines the outcome. The artist can start with line, or they can start with value, or they can start with texture, but always, one must start.

I hope you enjoy, and that you try to create your own stick figures with Simplicity in Mind.....

Julia Trops

OTHER THOUGHTS...

Many members of LIvessence did consider submitting for the show. Some of the feedback we heard included things like, I am not interested, to I don't see the point, to how can you simplify the human body? We asked for comments from those members who did not submit:

Lauri Copeman:
www.lauricopeman.com

"In my quest to honor the 2010 theme of Stick Figures, I found myself in an artistic dilemma -- either fulfill the vision of Livessence or fulfill the visions of my own Essence. My visions are voluptuous, meaty, and emotionally weighted. I struggled hard. I made three attempts, but they were not really in my heart and therefore did not translate into work I could call my own. For me, art must be made by the heart first and the hand second and, though I badly wanted to participate in the 2010 Livessence exhibits, my heart just would not cooperate."

Jesai Chantler
www.spirit-forces.com

"A lot of frustration seems to build around getting proportions, light and textures to harmonize and become believable and grounded. Its not just the figure that wants to be captured but the science of breath and the containment of the body and the laws of gravity. To me its not just art or drawing its also science."

Sydney Boultbee

"I am a new member to Livessence. I drive up from Penticton once a week for this chance to sketch from life. The models are excellent. The room provided has good space and light. It is a valuable learning experience for me. The camaraderie of the other artists is an aid to inspiration also."